Growing Your Business

Growing Your Business

Making Human Resources Work for You

Robert A. Baron and Scott Shane

business**expert**
Press

Growing Your Business

First published in 2008 by
Business Expert Press, LLC
222 East 46th Street, New York, NY 10017
www.businessexpertpress.com

ISBN-13: 978-1-60649-001-3 (paperback)
ISBN-10: 1-60649-001-X (paperback)

ISBN-13: 978-1-60649-003-7 (e-book)
ISBN-10: 1-60649-003-6 (e-book)

DOI 10.4128/9781606490037

A publication in the Entrepreneurship and Small Business Management collection

Collection ISSN (print) 1946-5653
Collection ISSN (electronic) 1946-5661

Cover design by Artistic Group—Monroe, NY
Interior design by Scribe, Inc.

First edition: October 2008

10 9 8 7 6 5 4 3 2 1

Printed in the United States of America.

Abstract

This book explains why you should grow your business and describes some of the major challenges of growth. It identifies several strategies that enhance the growth of new firms. It explains how you can select high-performing employees and describes various ways of enhancing employees' motivation and commitment, including the use of pay systems that help to retain high-performing employees. It describes various techniques you can use to increase trust in your new venture and explains why it is important for you to match your leadership style to the situations you face in your new venture.

Keywords

Entrepreneurship, growth, human resources

Contents

Introduction

Many venture capitalists are fond of saying that the jockey is more important than the horse, implying that the key dimension of a new venture that influences its ability to grow and prosper is the quality of the management team. While we are not sure that the management team of a venture is more important than the business opportunity in growing a business, we believe that the success of any new venture depends, to an important degree, on the knowledge, skills, talents, and abilities of its cofounders—plus those brought to it by initial employees. Therefore, to have a high-growth company, you need to put together the right human resources—the founding team and key hires. In this book, we explain how to do that.

Choosing excellent cofounders and management team members and developing good working relationships with them are complex tasks requiring considerable effort. How, then, can entrepreneurs assemble the human resources needed to launch a successful new venture? To answer this question in a useful way, we will consider four closely related topics.

First, we will examine the issue of *complementarity* versus *similarity*: Should entrepreneurs choose cofounders who are similar to themselves in various respects or those who are different in complementary ways, providing what they themselves lack in terms of knowledge, skills, or abilities? As we will note later in this discussion, both similarity and complementarity offer advantages, but we believe that emphasizing complementarity might, in many instances, be a somewhat better strategy because it provides new ventures with a strong and diverse base of human resources. In any case, the process of choosing appropriate cofounders should certainly start with a careful *self-assessment* by prospective entrepreneurs. The reason for this requirement can be stated simply: In a very real sense, it is impossible for entrepreneurs to know what they need from cofounders unless they (the entrepreneurs) know what they already have. Second, after considering why and how entrepreneurs should engage in careful self-assessment, we will examine the task of actually choosing cofounders. This requires skill at assessing others accurately and is far trickier than you might at first imagine. Most people are quite adept at managing their images and appearing to be what they are not, so being able to cut through such tactics is a skill worth developing. Third, we will turn to the issue of establishing effective working relationships with cofounders and new employees. This requires such preliminary steps as a clear division of roles and obligations, plus careful attention to basic principles of fairness and effective communication. Fourth, we will take a look at human resources beyond the founding team—how new ventures recruit the talented people they need and whether these people should be temporary or permanent employees.

Initially, entrepreneurs seek to *attract*, *motivate*, and *retain* high-quality people themselves—they want to choose everyone who joins their teams and to play a central role in motivating and retaining these people. But at some point, they must entrust these tasks to others. If that is the case, then why should you, as current or future entrepreneurs, be interested in these tasks? After all, you will ultimately turn them over to others. We think the answer involves three major points. First, the process through which entrepreneurs delegate these "people" tasks to others is gradual rather than sudden. Thus, information on how to accomplish them skillfully is useful to entrepreneurs during the early phases of their new ventures' growth, when they *will* be performing them. Second, most entrepreneurs want to place their personal stamps on their companies, and one important way of doing this is to play an active role in establishing the *systems* through which first-rate employees are recruited, motivated, and retained. Third, when they delegate these tasks to others, entrepreneurs need to choose these people well; and one way of assuring that this occurs is to understand just what these individuals will do. In sum, we think there are *several* reasons why it is important for you to understand the nature of these tasks (recruiting, motivating, and retaining excellent employees) and we will provide you with an overview of key factors relating to them. Our goal is certainly *not* to turn you into an expert on key aspects of human resource management; reaching that goal requires several years of specialized training. But we do want to arm you with basic information that we believe you will find valuable over and over again as you seek to enhance the growth of your new venture, and so move toward achieving your personal dreams and goals.

Similarity Versus Complementarity: Know Thyself

It is a basic fact of life that people feel most comfortable with, and tend to like, others who are similar to themselves in various ways.[1] In fact, a very large body of evidence points to two intriguing conclusions regarding the appeal of similarity: (a) almost any kind of similarity will do—similarity with respect to attitudes and values, demographic factors (e.g., age, gender, occupation, or ethnic background), shared interests—almost anything; and (b) such effects are both general and strong. For example, similarity has been found to influence the outcome of employment interviews and performance ratings: In general, the more similar job applicants are to the people who interview them, the more likely they are to be hired. Correspondingly, the more similar employees are to their managers, the higher the ratings they receive from them.[2] You can probably guess why similarity is so appealing: When people are alike on various dimensions, they are more comfortable in each other's presence, feel that they know each other better, and are more confident that they will be able to predict each other's future reactions and behavior. In short, everything else being equal, we tend to associate with, choose as friends or cofounders, and even marry people who are similar to ourselves in many respects.

Entrepreneurs are definitely no exception to this *similarity-leads-to-liking* rule. In fact, most tend to select people whose background, training, and experience is highly similar to their own. This is far from surprising: People from similar backgrounds "speak the same language"—they can converse more readily and smoothly than people from very different backgrounds; and often, they already know one another because they have attended the same schools or worked for the same companies. The overall result is that many new ventures are started by teams of entrepreneurs from the same fields or occupations: Engineers tend to work with engineers, entrepreneurs with a marketing or sales background tend to work with others from these fields, scientists tend to work with other scientists, and so on.

In one sense, this is an important "plus": As we will note in a later section, effective communication is a key ingredient in good working relations, so the fact that birds of a feather tend to flock together in starting new ventures offers obvious advantages. On the debit side of the ledger, however, the tendency for entrepreneurs to choose cofounders whose background and training is highly similar to their own has several serious drawbacks. The most important of these centers around *redundancy*: The more similar people are, the greater the degree to which their knowledge, training, skills, and aptitudes overlap. For example, consider a group of engineers who start a company to develop a new product. All have technical expertise, and this is extremely useful in terms of designing a product that actually works. But because they are all engineers, they have little knowledge about marketing, legal matters, or regulations concerning employees' health and safety. Further, they might know very little about writing an effective business plan, which is often crucial for obtaining required financial resources and determining how to operate a company effectively. Moreover, although all of them have excellent quantitative skills, they are not proficient at preparing written documents or "selling" their ideas; as is often the case with people from a technical or scientific background, they are better with numbers than words. Further, since all were trained in the same field (and might even have studied at the same school), they have overlapping social networks: They tend to know the same people and hence have a limited range of contacts from whom they can obtain needed resources—information, financial support, and so on.

By now the main point should be clear: What this particular team of entrepreneurs—or any other team—needs for success is a very wide range of information, skills, aptitudes, and abilities. And this is less likely to be present when all members of the founding team are highly similar to one another in important ways. Ideally, what one team member lacks, one or more others can provide because the team can pool its knowledge and expertise. For entrepreneurs who are assembling their founding teams, rule number one is this: Do not yield to the temptation to work solely with people whose background, training, and experience is highly similar to your own. Doing so will be easy and pleasant in many ways, but it will not provide the rich foundation of human resources that the new venture needs.

Self-Assessment: Knowing What You Have Helps to Determine What You Need

Now that we have clarified the dangers associated with the potential downside of choosing to work exclusively with cofounders similar to oneself, we will take a step back and briefly examine a related issue: the importance of an accurate self-assessment in this process. As we noted earlier, it is difficult, if not impossible, to know what you need from prospective cofounders without first understanding what you, yourself, bring to the table. For this reason, a crucial initial step for all entrepreneurs—one that they should perform *before* beginning the task of assembling required human resources (cofounders or additional employees)—is a careful *self-assessment*, an inventory of the knowledge, experience, training, and motives that they themselves possess and can contribute to the new venture.

This is far from a simple task: The dictum "know thyself" sounds straightforward, but in reality, it is exceedingly difficult to put into actual practice. There are two major reasons why this is so. First, we are often unaware of at least some of the factors that affect our behavior. The powerful effect of similarity, described above, is a prime example of this fact. Often, people like others, including prospective cofounders, because of subtle similarities—they are alike in various ways but are not fully aware of these similarities. In short, they know that they like each other and find it pleasant to work together but they do not really know why! To the extent that we are unaware of the factors that influence our behavior and reactions, the task of knowing ourselves becomes complex.

Second, and perhaps more important, we do not gain knowledge of our abilities, or even attitudes, directly through self-reflection. Rather, we gradually gain insight into these important aspects of ourselves through our relations with others. Only other people—and their reactions to us—can tell us how intelligent, energetic, charming, or well-informed about various topics we are. There are no direct physical measures of these and many other attributes, so we have to gather them, gradually, from what other people tell us, directly or indirectly.

Although the task of acquiring clear self-knowledge is a complex one, we *can* perform it quite well—if we take the trouble to do so. There are concrete steps you, as a prospective entrepreneur, can take to develop an accurate view of your own human capital—the resources you bring to any new venture you choose to launch. You can complete several key portions of this personal inventory yourself, but for others, you will need the help of people who know you well—and hence, can provide insights you cannot readily acquire alone. Remember that the reason for engaging in this activity is to understand what you already have—your own human capital—so that you can determine what you need from other individuals, including potential cofounders.

Knowledge Base. This is a good place to begin because it is something you can do alone. Ask yourself the following questions: "What do I know?" "What information and knowledge do I bring to the new venture?" Here, your education and experience are directly relevant and can suggest what you know and what you do not know and therefore need to acquire from others, including potential cofounders.

Specific Skills. Quite apart from your knowledge base are specific skills—proficiencies that enable you to perform certain tasks well. Are you very good with numbers? Adept at making oral presentations? Good with people? Everyone has a unique set of skills, and you should try to understand—and inventory—yours as a preliminary step in developing your new venture.

Motives. This is not only more difficult but also quite important. Why do you want to start a new venture? Because you like a challenge? Because you fervently believe in your new product? To earn a huge fortune? To escape from corporate life and become self-employed? You can hold all of these motives at the same time, but it is useful to ponder their relative importance to you because if your personal motives do not match those of potential cofounders, you might be laying the foundation for serious future problems.

Commitment. This is related to motivation but not identical to it. Commitment refers to the desire to see things through (i.e., to continue even in the face of adversity) and to reach your personal goals relating to the new venture (e.g., those listed under motives). Recent findings indicate that this is an important factor in new venture success.[3]

Similarity or Complementarity: A Final Word

So which should you seek in prospective team members, similarity or complementarity? The answer depends largely on the dimensions you are considering. Complementarity is very important with respect to knowledge, skills, and experience. In order to succeed, new ventures must acquire a rich and useful inventory of human resources. Choosing cofounders whose knowledge and experience complement your own can be very useful in attaining this important goal. On the other hand, similarity, too, offers benefits: It enhances ease of communication and facilitates good personal relationships. And similarity with respect to motives is very important: If the cofounders of a new venture have sharply contrasting motives or goals, conflict between them is almost certain to develop.

Overall, then, we suggest a balanced approach: Focus primarily on complementarity with respect to knowledge, skills, and experience, but bring similarity into the picture with respect to motives.[4] Doing so will provide good symmetry between acquiring the broad range of human resources that new ventures require and establishing a good working environment in which all members of the founding team can work hard to convert their vision into reality.

Good luck with your personal inventory—and with the task of choosing excellent cofounders. And as you proceed, keep the words of Lao Tzu, a philosopher of ancient China, firmly in mind: "He who knows others is clever; He who knows himself has discernment."

Choosing Cofounders: Maximizing the New Venture's Human Resources

As we noted in the preceding section, it is considerably harder to "know thyself" than you might at first assume. With a little hard work, however, it *is* possible to formulate an accurate inventory of your own human capital—what you bring to the new venture in terms of knowledge, skills, experience, and personal characteristics. This, in turn, can help you determine what you need from other people (e.g., cofounders and employees) in terms of these basic dimensions. Once you have drawn a bead on this issue, though, things do *not* necessarily get simpler, because knowing what you need is no guarantee that you will find it—or that you will recognize it when you do. Superb cofounders do not appear, conveniently, just when you need them. On the contrary, identifying such people usually requires considerable work. Accomplishing this task is very worthwhile, because choosing badly can have disastrous consequences. These points raise an important, practical question: How should entrepreneurs go about selecting potential cofounders—what guidelines should they use in assembling the human resources required for their new ventures? Answering this question involves many activities, but perhaps most central among these is developing skill at what is known as social perception—the process through which we come to know and understand other people.[1]

This is a key task because unless we form accurate perceptions of others, it is impossible to determine whether, and to what extent, they possess the knowledge, skills, and characteristics we seek. For this reason, developing skill at this task is very useful for entrepreneurs.[2] Unfortunately, perceiving others accurately is more difficult than it sounds because other people do not always portray themselves accurately. On the contrary, they often seek to disguise their true feelings or motives, and frequently seek to present themselves in a favorable light. If we accept these external masks at face value, we can be seriously misled. To perceive others accurately, therefore, we must learn to be adept at distinguishing reality from image where other people are concerned. In this respect, developing skill at dealing with two related issues—impression management and deception—is extremely useful.

Impression Management: The Fine Art of Looking Good—and How to Recognize It

At one time or another, virtually everyone engages in efforts to make a good first impression—to present themselves in a favorable light.[3] To accomplish this goal, individuals use a wide range of tactics. Most of these, however, fall into two major categories: *self-enhancement*—efforts to increase their appeal to others—and *other-enhancement*—efforts to make the target person feel good in various ways.

Specific strategies of self-enhancement include efforts to boost one's physical appearance through style of dress, personal grooming, and the use of various "props."[4] Additional tactics of self-enhancement involve efforts to appear highly skilled or describing oneself in positive terms—such as explaining how the person engaging in impression management overcame daunting obstacles.

Turning to other-enhancement, individuals use many different tactics to induce positive moods and reactions in others. A large body of research findings suggests that such reactions, in turn, play an important role in getting other people to like you.[5] The most commonly used tactic of other-enhancement is *flattery*—making statements that praise the target person, his or her traits or accomplishments, or the organization with which the target person is associated.[6] Such tactics are often highly successful, provided that they are not overdone. Additional tactics of other-enhancement involve expressing agreement with the target person's views, showing a high degree of interest in the person, doing small favors for him or her, asking for his or her advice and feedback in some manner, or expressing liking nonverbally (e.g., through high levels of eye contact, nodding in agreement, and smiling).[7]

These are not the only strategies people use; for example, individuals sometimes employ *intimidation*—pretending to be dangerous or angry in order to wring concessions from others. This tactic does not generate positive reactions to the people using it, but it does often produce the results they desire. Have you ever known anyone who relies on this approach? Such people are far from rare, and they often enter meetings with an approach suggesting, "I'm mad as hell and I'm not going to take it anymore!" If this tactic is recognized for what it is, its impact is reduced; but for some people it works well in many situations.[8]

Do other tactics of impression management actually succeed? The answer provided by a growing body of literature is clear: yes, provided that they are used with skill and care. For example, one large-scale study involving more than 1,400 employees found that social skills (including impression management) were the single best predictor of job performance ratings and assessments of potential for promotion for employees in a wide range of jobs.[9] Overall, then, it appears that impression management tactics often do enhance the appeal of people who use them effectively. We should hasten to add, however, that the use of these tactics involves potential pitfalls: If they are overused or used ineffectively they can backfire and produce negative rather than positive reactions from others. For example, people often form very negative impressions of others who play up to their superiors while treating subordinates with disdain and contempt—sometimes known as the slime effect.[10] The moral of these findings is clear: Although tactics of impression management often succeed, this is not always the case, and sometimes, they can boomerang, adversely affecting reactions to the person who uses them.

By now, it should be obvious that being able to "cut through" these various tactics of impression management is very important for prospective entrepreneurs engaged in the task of choosing prospective cofounders and initial employees. Accepting others' statements about their skills, experience, and past accomplishments without *due diligence* (carefully checking on the accuracy of such information) can lead entrepreneurs to form inflated views of the people who are using such tactics. Similarly, failing to recognize flattery, exaggerated agreement or similarity, and related tactics can lead entrepreneurs to go with their hearts instead of their heads in assembling the initial teams for their new ventures. Developing the ability to recognize such tactics when they are used requires considerable practice, but simply calling them to your attention is useful; some research findings indicate that where impression management is concerned, to be forewarned is to be forearmed. Certainly, we are not suggesting that you adopt a cynical approach to other people—that, too, can be harmful. But accepting the information or outward façade presented by strangers without due diligence is not only naïve; it can also be very costly to the fortunes of a new venture.

Utilizing the New Venture's Human Resources: Building Strong Working Relationships Among the Founding Team

Assembling the resources needed to perform a task is an essential first step; indeed, there is no sense in starting unless the required resources are available—or easily obtained "on the fly." But this is only the beginning; the task itself must then be performed. The same principle holds true for new ventures: Assembling the necessary human resources—an appropriate pool of knowledge, experience, skills, and abilities—is only the beginning. The people who constitute the founding team must then work together in an effective manner if the new venture is to succeed. Unfortunately, this key point is often overlooked, or at least given very little attention, by new entrepreneurs. They are so focused on the opportunity that they have identified and wish to develop that they pay scant attention to building strong working relationships with one another—working relationships that will permit the new venture to utilize its human resources to the fullest.

Growing evidence suggests that such relationships are an essential ingredient in new ventures' success.[11] For example, in one recent study of 70 new ventures, higher levels of cohesion among the founding team (positive feelings toward one another) were strongly associated with superior financial performance by these new ventures.[12] In view of such evidence, a key question arises: How can strong working relationships between founding team members be encouraged? While there is no simple answer to this question, there are three factors that appear to play a crucial role: (a) a clear initial assignment of roles (responsibilities and authority) for all team members, (b) careful attention to the basic issue of perceived fairness, and (c) development of effective patterns and styles of communication (especially with respect to feedback) among team members.

Roles: The Clearer the Better

A major source of conflict in many organizations is uncertainty concerning two issues: responsibility and jurisdiction. Disagreements—often harsh and angry ones—easily develop over the question of who is supposed to be accountable for what (responsibility), and over the question of who has the authority to make decisions and choose among alternative courses of action (jurisdiction).[13] One effective way of avoiding such problems is through the clear definition of roles—the set of behaviors that individuals occupying specific positions within a group are expected to perform, and the authority or jurisdiction that they will wield. Once established, clear roles can be very useful.

For example, consider a new biotechnology venture with two cofounders. One holds an MD and is a practicing physician with a specialty in cardiology, while the other holds an MBA. To maximize their effectiveness as a team, these individuals should negotiate clearly defined roles at the outset. One possibility: The MD runs the laboratory, since it is conducting medical research and he is intimately familiar with the rules and regulations governing such activities; he is also responsible for interfacing with other MDs and for choosing the drugs on which to focus—after all, he is an expert on the symptoms and causes of various medical conditions. The other founder, in contrast, handles business-related aspects of the company (e.g., purchase and maintenance of equipment, setting up the company's computer systems) and, because of his business expertise, oversees hiring of new personnel and financial tasks ranging from securing new capital to maintaining required records. If these roles are specified clearly in advance, the cofounders will truly work in a complementary manner—each will provide unique skills, experience, and knowledge that the other does not possess, or possesses to a lesser degree. The result? The company will operate smoothly and efficiently.

Imagine, however, that the MD decides that he should take an active hand with respect to the company's finances. This would not be surprising because bright, talented people often think it will be fun to do something that they have not done before. Since the MD lacks knowledge in this area, he will have to spend considerable time acquiring a working knowledge of financial statements, tax regulations, and so on. This is inefficient. Moreover, his partner, who holds an MBA, might find this to be irritating at best and downright insulting at worst. The result? Conflict between the cofounders will occur, and the company will operate at lower efficiency.

The moral is clear: Once the founding team has come together to form the new venture, its members should stick to the principle of complementarity. This implies dividing responsibilities and authority in accordance with each founder's expertise and knowledge. Anything else might well prove costly and detract from the new venture's success. This sounds very simple, but the sad fact is that many entrepreneurs are highly energetic, capable people, used to "running the show" in their own lives. Unless they can learn to coordinate with their cofounders, though, they might run the risk of seriously weakening their own companies.

Perceived Fairness: An Elusive but Essential Component

Try this simple exercise: Think back over your life and remember a specific occasion when you worked with one or more persons on a project. The context is unimportant—it can be any kind of project you wish—but try to recall an incident in which the outcome was positive; the project was a success. Now, divide 100 points between yourself and your partners according to how large a contribution each person made to the project. Next comes the key question: How did you divide the points? If you are like most people, you gave yourself more points than your partners. (For example, if you had one partner, you took more than 50 points; if you had two partners, you took more than 33.3 points, and so on.)

Now, by way of contrast, try to recall another incident—one in which you also worked with partners but in which the outcome was negative; the project failed. Once again divide 100 points between yourself and your partners, according to how large a contribution each person made to the project and its outcome. In this case, you might well have given them more points than yourself. If you showed this pattern, welcome to the club: You are demonstrating a very powerful human tendency, often known as the self-serving bias. This is the tendency to attribute successful outcomes largely to internal causes (e.g., our own efforts, talents, or abilities) but unsuccessful ones largely to external causes (e.g., the failings or negligence of others and factors beyond our control).[14] This bias has been found to be a strong one, and it has serious implications for any situation in which people work together to achieve important goals. Specifically, it often leads all the people involved to conclude that somehow they have not been treated fairly. Why? Because since each participant in the relationship tends to accentuate his or her own contributions and minimize those of others, that person usually concludes that he or she is receiving less of the available rewards than is justified. Further, since each person has the same perception, the result is often friction and conflict between the people involved.

In other words, this tendency raises thorny questions relating to perceived fairness—a key issue for entrepreneurs. Because of the self-serving bias (and other factors), we all have a tendency to assume that we are receiving less than we deserve in almost any situation. In other words, we perceive that the balance between what we contribute and what we receive is less favorable than it is for other people. In specific terms, we perceive that the ratio between what we are receiving and what we are contributing is smaller than that for others. In general, we prefer this ratio to be the same for all, so that the larger any person's contributions, the larger his or her rewards—a principle known as distributive justice. Most people accept this principle as valid, but the self-serving bias leads us to cognitively inflate our own contributions— and hence to conclude that, in fact, we are not being treated fairly.

What do people do when they perceive that the distribution of rewards is unfair? The answer is many different things, none of which are beneficial to a new venture. The most obvious tactic is to demand a larger share; since others do not view these demands as legitimate, conflict is the likely outcome. Another approach is to reduce one's contributions—to reduce effort or shirk responsibility. This, too, can be highly detrimental to the success of a new venture. An even more damaging reaction is to withdraw—either physically or psychologically. Disaffected cofounders sometimes pull out of new ventures, taking their experience, knowledge, and skills with them. If they are essential members of the team, this can mark the beginning of the end for the ventures in question.

All this is bad enough, but even worse is the recent finding that while people tend to focus relatively little attention on the issue of fairness when things are going well (e.g., they are getting along well with their cofounders), they devote increasing attention to this issue when things begin to go badly.[15] In short, when a new venture is succeeding and reaching its goals, members of the founding team might show little concern over distributive justice. If things go badly, however, they begin to focus increasing attention on this issue—thus intensifying this interpersonal friction.

Given the existence of this cycle, it is truly crucial for the founding teams of new ventures to consider the issue of perceived fairness very carefully. This implies that they should discuss this issue regularly to assure that as roles, responsibilities, and contributions to the new venture change (which they inevitably will do over time), adjustments are made with respect to equity, status, and other rewards to reflect these changes. This is a difficult task since all members will tend to accentuate their own contributions (recall the powerful self-serving bias). But since the alternative is the very real risk of tension and conflict between the founding team members and since conflict is often a major waste of time and energy,[16] it is certainly a task worth performing well—and one that will help the new venture utilize its human resources to the fullest extent.

One more point: Issues of fairness arise not only between cofounders but also between companies that form business alliances. Such alliances can often be extremely helpful to new ventures, but in order to survive, they must be perceived as fair and mutually beneficial by both sides. Here is one example of an alliance that has been very successful. 8minuteDating is a young company with an idea that has taken the matchmaking industry by storm. At 8minuteDating events, single men and women gather at a restaurant, chat in couples for 8 minutes, and then move on to the next table, where they meet another person. This allows each person participating in the event to meet many potential partners in one evening instead of just one, as is the case in traditional dating. After the event is over, couples who like each other can meet again. Recently, 8minute-Dating has formed an alliance with Tele-Publishing International (TPI), a company that runs the personal ad pages for 550 newspapers in the United States.

How did this occur? The founder of 8minuteDating, Tom Jafee, learned that Adam Segal, an executive with TPI, was having dinner with his mother at a restaurant where an 8minuteDating event was being held. Jafee introduced himself, and the two entrepreneurs quickly realized that they could form a mutually beneficial alliance: TPI would advertise 8minuteDating in its personal columns, and 8minuteDating events would distribute free coupons and sponsor other promotions to encourage its customers to try the personal ads. The alliance has worked like a charm: Both companies have benefited considerably. Both see it as fair and as helping them to attain their major goals. As Segal puts it, "The beauty of our alliance is that it can expand with 8minuteDating's growth. Every time they start events in a new city, TPI will already be there with our personal ads in the newspapers. Talk about a match made in heaven."[17] So if you consider forming an alliance with another company, be sure to devote careful attention to the question of fairness: Alliances that are not perceived as meeting this essential criterion are unlikely to survive.

Effective Communication

Perceived unfairness is not the only cause of costly conflicts between members of a new venture's founding team. Another major factor involves faulty styles of communication. Unfortunately, individuals often communicate with others in a way that angers or annoys the recipients, even when it is not their intention to do so. This happens in many different ways, but one of the most common—and important—involves delivering feedback, especially negative feedback, in an inappropriate manner. In essence, there is only one truly rational reason for delivering negative feedback to another person: to help that person improve. Yet, people often deliver negative feedback for other reasons: to put the recipient in his or her "place," to cause him to lose face in front of others, to express anger and hostility, and so on. The result of such negative feedback is that the recipient experiences anger or humiliation in turn, and this can be the basis for smoldering resentment and long-lasting grudges.[18] When negative feedback is delivered in an informal context rather than formally (e.g., as part of a written performance review), it is known as criticism, and research suggests that such feedback can take two distinct forms: constructive criticism, which is truly designed to help the recipient improve, and destructive criticism, which is perceived—rightly so—as a form of hostility or attack.

What makes criticism constructive or destructive in nature? Constructive criticism is considerate of the recipient's feelings, does not contain threats, is timely (i.e., occurs at an appropriate point in time), does not attribute blame to the recipient, is specific in content, and offers concrete suggestions for improvement. Destructive criticism, in contrast, is harsh, contains threats, is not timely, blames the recipient for negative outcomes, is not specific in content, and offers no concrete ideas for improvement.

Research findings indicate that destructive criticism is truly destructive: It generates strong negative reactions in recipients and can initiate a vicious cycle of anger, the desire for revenge, and subsequent conflict. The message for entrepreneurs is clear: Effective communication between cofounders is one essential ingredient in establishing and maintaining effective working relationships. If this is lacking, serious problems might result. For example, consider a new venture started by partners who have followed the complementarity principle: one is an engineer and the other has a background in marketing. Although the marketing cofounder has selected a partner carefully, she harbors negative feelings about engineers. ("They never think about people!") As a result, she criticizes the engineer's designs for new products harshly. The engineer is offended by this treatment, so he begins to make changes in the company's products without informing his cofounder. Since the marketing entrepreneur does not know about these changes, she cannot get customer input before they are made. The result? The company's products bomb in the marketplace, and soon the new venture is in deep trouble. This is just one example of how faulty communication between members of the founding team can produce disastrous effects. The main point should be clear: Strong efforts to attain good, constructive communication between cofounders are very worthwhile.

Is all conflict between founding cofounders bad? Absolutely not. Conflict between team members can, if it is focused on specific issues rather than personalities and is held within rational bounds, be very useful.

Such "rational" conflict can help to focus attention on important issues, motivate both sides to understand each other's view more clearly, and can, by encouraging both sides to carefully consider all assumptions, lead to better decisions.[19] In sum, conflict between founding team members is not necessarily a bad thing. Rather, it—like all other aspects of the new venture's operations—should be carefully managed so that benefits are maximized and costs held to a minimum. Overall, strong and effective working relationships between founding members are a powerful asset to any new venture, so efforts to foster them should be high on every founding team's Must-Do list.

Expanding the New Venture's Human Resources: Beyond the Founding Team

The founding team of any new venture is a key component of its human resources. A first-rate group of founders brings a wealth of knowledge, experience, skills, and commitment to their company.[1] Further, as common sense would suggest, the larger the founding team and the more varied the experience of its members (the principle of complementarity), the greater the likelihood that the new venture will succeed—specifically, the greater the new venture's chances of survival[2] and the faster its rate of growth.[3] But no matter how excellent a new venture's founding team is, it cannot possibly supply all required resources or all forms of information. At the very least, new ventures often require the services of experts from outside the company—such as lawyers, accountants, or engineers. And if the new venture is successful in obtaining financing and in building a customer base, the need for additional human resources in the form of employees beyond the founding team might soon become apparent. This raises several important and related questions: (a) How can new ventures succeed in obtaining the employees they need? (b) How many should they hire? and (c) Should these be temporary or permanent employees? Research on these questions provides relatively clear and informative answers.

Obtaining Excellent Employees: The Role of Social Networks

New ventures face serious obstacles with respect to attracting outstanding employees. As new companies, they are relatively unknown to potential employees and cannot offer the legitimacy or security of established firms. Thus, they enter the market for human resources with important disadvantages. How do start-up companies overcome these difficulties? They do so largely through the use of social networks. In other words, they tend to hire people they know either directly, from personal contact, or indirectly, through recommendations from people they do know and trust.[4] This is helpful to new ventures in several ways.

First, by hiring people they know (often, family members, friends, or former coworkers), entrepreneurs are able to acquire human resources quickly, without the necessity for long and costly searches. Second, since they know the people whom they hire either directly or indirectly, it is easier for entrepreneurs to convince these individuals of the value of the opportunity that they are pursuing. Third, new ventures often lack clearly established rules or a well-defined culture; having direct or indirect ties with new employees makes the task of integrating them into this somewhat loose and changing structure easier.

In sum, new ventures generally hire people known to the founding entrepreneurs either directly or indirectly and, in this way, are able to expand their bases of human resources in a relatively rapid and cost-effective manner.

Is Bigger Necessarily Better? Number of Employees as a Factor in New Venture Growth

New ventures face many difficult questions as they grow and develop, but one of the most perplexing among these concerns is the number of employees they should hire. Adding employees—expanding the new venture's human resources—offers obvious advantages. New employees are a source of information, skills, and energy; also, the more employees a new venture has, the greater the number and larger the size of the projects it can undertake. As we noted earlier, there is little doubt that in many contexts people working together in a coordinated manner can accomplish far more than individuals working alone. But adding employees to a new venture has an obvious downside, too. Employees add to the new venture's fixed expenses and raise many complex issues relating to their own health and safety, which must be carefully considered. In a sense, expanding the company's workforce is a double-edged sword, and the results of expanding the number of employees can truly be mixed.

Overall, however, existing evidence suggests that on balance, the benefits of increasing the number of employees outweigh the costs. New ventures that start with more employees have a greater chance of surviving than those that begin with a smaller number.[5] Similarly, companies with more employees have higher rates of growth than those with fewer employees.[6] Profitability, too, is positively related to the size of new ventures. For example, the greater the number of employees, the larger the earnings of new ventures and the greater the income generated by them for their founders.[7]

We should hasten to note that these findings are all correlational in nature; they indicate that the number of employees is related, in a positive manner, to several measures of new ventures' success. They do not, however, indicate that hiring new employees causes such success. In fact, both number of employees and various measures of financial success might stem from other, underlying factors, such as the quality of the opportunity being developed, commitment and talent of the founding team, and even general economic conditions. (It is often easier to hire good employees at reasonable cost when the economy is weak than when it is strong.) So the relationship between new-venture size (number of employees) and new-venture success should be approached with a degree of caution. Still, having said this, it is clear that human resources are a key ingredient in the success of start-up companies; to the extent that a new venture can afford to expand its workforce, doing so might be an effective strategy.

Should New Ventures Hire Temporary or Permanent Employees? Commitment Versus Cost

Achieving an appropriate balance between costs and number of new employees is not the only issue facing new ventures where expanding their workforces is concerned; in addition, they must determine whether new employees should be hired on a temporary or permanent basis. Again, there are advantages and disadvantages to both strategies. Temporary employees reduce fixed costs and provide for a great deal of flexibility; they can be hired and released as the fortunes of the venture dictate.

Furthermore, hiring temporary employees permits the new venture to secure specialized knowledge or skills that might be required for a specific project; when the project is completed, the temporary employees depart, thus reducing costs.

On the other side of the coin, there are several disadvantages associated with temporary employees. First, they might lack the commitment and motivation of permanent employees. After all, they know that they have been hired on a contract basis for a specified period of time (though this can often be extended), so they have little feeling of commitment to the new venture; in a sense, they are visitors, not permanent residents. In addition, there is the real risk that temporary employees will acquire valuable information about the company or its opportunity and then carry this to potential competitors. Certainly, that is a serious danger for any new venture. Permanent employees, in contrast, tend to be more strongly committed and motivated with respect to the new venture, and are less likely to leave—especially if they gain an equity stake in the company.

The choice between temporary and permanent employees is a difficult one. Which is preferable seems to depend, to a large extent, on specific conditions faced by a new venture, such as the industry in which it operates or the opportunity it is attempting to exploit. In situations where flexibility and speed of acquiring new sets of knowledge and expertise are crucial (e.g., among software start-up companies), temporary employees might be very beneficial.[8] In situations where employee commitment and retention are more important (e.g., employees rapidly acquire skills and knowledge that increase their value to the new venture), then focusing on a permanent workforce might be preferable.[9]

Recruiting and Selecting High-Performing Employees

Earlier in this book, we suggested that new ventures are at a serious disadvantage when they enter the labor market to attract high-quality employees. Because they are new, they are relatively unknown to potential employees and cannot offer the security or "brand familiarity" of established firms. Although there is currently little direct evidence on this issue, it seems reasonable to suggest that unless new ventures succeed in overcoming these obstacles, they might be doomed to failure—after all, they cannot grow if they fail to attract and retain essential and dedicated employees. How, then, should entrepreneurs approach this important task? To provide you with some useful guidelines, we will consider two basic questions: (a) Where should entrepreneurs search for high-quality employees? and (b) What specific techniques should they use to identify the best among them?

The Search for High-Performing Employees: Knowing What You Need and Where to Look

There is an old saying: It's hard to get somewhere unless you know where you want to go. In other words, it is hard to reach a goal unless you have defined it clearly. That is certainly true with respect to hiring high-quality employees. Before beginning a search for such people, it is crucial to first determine just what it is that your new venture is seeking. In the field of human resource management, this implies two preliminary tasks: (a) a job analysis—determining just what the job involves and what it requires in terms of specific knowledge, skills, and abilities[1]—and (b) formulation of a clear job description—an overview of what the job involves in terms of its duties, responsibilities, and working conditions. In large companies, job analyses can be very detailed and lead to highly specific job descriptions, but for entrepreneurs, especially in the very hectic early days of a new venture, when founders have to do virtually everything, it is usually sufficient for them to simply have a clear idea of what the person or persons they are seeking will actually do, and a brief written description of the major duties and tasks that they will perform.

Why are these initial steps so important? Because they provide a basis for choosing among potential employees, for selecting the ones most likely to succeed in a specific job. The best choice, all other factors being equal, is the person whose knowledge, skills, and abilities provide the closest match to the requirements of the job. If they have not conducted a job analysis and formulated a clear job description for a particular position, entrepreneurs (or the people to whom they delegate this task) will still need to proceed with choosing among potential employees; it is a task that must be accomplished. However, it will be more difficult for them to make these choices on the basis of job requirements. Instead, for example, they might choose the people they find most congenial or attractive, or applicants who somehow "stand out from the crowd" rather than the person best qualified for the job. For this reason, it is best to formulate a clear idea of the specific requirements of any job before beginning the search-and-selection process.

Having said that, we should add that in some industries—those that are on the cutting edge of technological advancement, such as biotechnology—it might be very difficult to specify the requirements of various positions very precisely because conditions are changing so rapidly that the tasks people perform, too, will certainly change. But insofar as conditions will permit, it is a good idea to first determine, as precisely as possible, what's needed before beginning the search for new employees.

Once the task of specifying precisely what is needed—what skills and abilities new employees will provide to the growing venture—has been completed, the search for these people can begin. Earlier, we noted that new ventures often fill their initial needs for additional human resources largely through their founders' social networks. In other words, they tend to hire people they know either directly, from personal contact, or indirectly, through recommendations from people they do know and trust.[2] Here we will expand on those comments by indicating that referrals from current or former employees are often especially helpful in this regard. If new ventures continue to grow, however, these sources might soon prove to be inadequate; they simply do not produce a sufficient number of potential employees or ones with the full array of knowledge and skills the new venture needs.

At that point, entrepreneurs must expand their searches. One way of doing so is through advertisements in carefully selected publications. For example, ads might be placed in trade journals that reach specific, targeted audiences. Since new ventures usually lack the resources to screen large numbers of applicants, it is generally less useful for them to advertise in mass-circulation outlets such as large local newspapers (although, of course, there might be exceptions to this general rule). Other useful sources include visits to college and university employment centers; here, once again, it is possible to specify job requirements quite precisely and to be reasonably certain of interviewing only individuals whose qualifications match these closely. In recent years, Internet sites have been developed to assist companies in finding employees, and potential employees in finding jobs (e.g., CareerBuilder.com, Headhunters.com, and Monster.com).

Entrepreneurs should not overlook current customers as a potential source of new employees. Customers know the new ventures' products and are familiar with its operations, so they can often be a very helpful source of referrals. Finally, professional "headhunters" are often helpful. Venture capitalists (VCs) often have working relationships with such firms to help the start-ups they fund obtain management talent. So this can be a very useful source for entrepreneurs who have obtained financial support from VCs. Together, the sources outlined here are often sufficient to provide growing new ventures with a pool of applicants from which they can choose. And that brings us to the next important step in the process: techniques for selecting the best people in this pool.

Selection: Techniques for Choosing the "Cream of the Crop"

Our experience tells us that in many cases, new ventures do a reasonably good job of assembling a pool of potential employees: Their social networks, current customers, and other sources yield a number of people who could, at first glance, be hired. Choosing among them, however, is another story. This is a difficult task under the best of conditions even in large organizations that have human resource departments with experts specifically trained to perform this task. (These are rarely found in companies that have fewer than several hundred employees.) Entrepreneurs, in contrast, often lack such specialized experience and, moreover, must try to fit the task of making these decisions into their extremely busy days. Furthermore, serious mistakes—hiring an incompetent or unethical person—are even more costly for new ventures, with their limited resources, than for large, preexisting companies. So how can entrepreneurs accomplish this task effectively? The answer, basically, is through a combination of several techniques.

First, it is essential for us to add a few words on the topics of reliability and validity, because these concepts are closely related to the question of selecting the best employees. Reliability refers to the extent to which measurements are consistent across time or between judges. For example, if you step on your bathroom scale this morning and it reads "150 pounds," but then you get back on it 10 minutes later and it reads, "140 pounds," you might question its reliability; your weight has not changed in 10 minutes, so the scale does not seem to be providing consistent measurements. (Perhaps it needs a new battery.) A good illustration of reliability across judges is the ratings given to champion figure skaters by a panel of judges. The more the judges agree, the more reliable (consistent) their ratings are viewed to be. In contrast to reliability, validity refers to the extent to which measurements actually reflect the underlying dimension to which they refer.

Reliability and validity are closely related to the task of selecting the best people for specific jobs; only selection tools or techniques that are both reliable and valid are useful for this purpose—and legal under existing laws (e.g., the Equal Employment Opportunity Commission's Americans with Disability Act). In fact, if the validity of any technique used for selection is doubtful, using that technique can result in costly lawsuits; keep this fact in mind if this is a type of trouble that you would rather avoid!

So where do various selection tools stand with respect to reliability and validity? Many, it turns out, are quite low on both of these dimensions. Letters of recommendation, for example, have been found to be almost totally unrelated to actual on-the-job performance, which means that they are very low in validity. Surprisingly, the same is true for standard employment interviews—the selection technique that is by far the most widely used. Traditional interviews, which are largely unstructured in nature and proceed in any way that the interviewer wishes, suffer from several major problems that tend to reduce their validity. For example, interviewers often make their decisions very early, after only a few minutes—well before they have had a chance to gather pertinent information about an applicant.[3] Second, if interviewers ask different questions of each applicant and allow the length of the interview to vary greatly, how can they later compare the various applicants in a systematic manner?[4] The answer is that they cannot, so validity suffers.

Additional problems involve the fact that interviewers, like everyone else, are subject to subtle forms of bias in the way that they perceive applicants. A large body of evidence indicates that attractive applicants, those who are similar to the interviewer in various respects (age, background, ethnic identity), and those who are good at impression management tend to have a major edge over applicants who are less attractive, less similar to the interviewer, and less skilled at impression management.[5] Such factors are largely unrelated to the ability of various persons to perform the jobs for which they are being interviewed, so this means that the validity of such interviews is questionable, at best.

Despite these drawbacks and despite the bizarre results that they often yield, most companies—including new ventures—continue to employ brief job interviews as the primary means through which they choose their employees. Why is this so? Probably because most people, including entrepreneurs, suffer from the illusion that they are highly skilled at social perception. In other words, they believe that they can form an accurate impression of others' major traits, motives, and talents on the basis of a brief conversation with them.[6] In fact, however, systematic research suggests that we are unduly optimistic in this regard: The task of assessing others is far more difficult, and subject to many more sources of error, than most people realize. Suffice it to say that we are generally less successful at this task than we believe and that this calls the validity of traditional job interviews into serious question.

Fortunately, the validity of interviews can be greatly improved by switching to what are known as structured interviews, in which all applicants are asked the same questions—those chosen carefully to be truly job-related. Some of the questions (situational questions) ask the applicants how they would respond to particular work situations (e.g., "What would you do if you ran out of supplies?"), while others focus on job knowledge (e.g., "How did you acquire the necessary information to complete a particular task?"). Additional questions focus on applicants' willingness to perform the job under current conditions (e.g., "What are your feelings about working overtime during very busy periods?") Empirical evidence suggests that structured interviews are, perhaps, the most valid technique for selecting employees: Different interviewers come up with similar ratings for the same applicants, and these ratings do predict on-the-job performance. So although they are not perfect, structured interviews offer a useful technique—one that can help entrepreneurs make the correct decisions when choosing among several applicants.

Another technique for selecting employees that is reasonably high in validity involves biodata—information about their backgrounds, experiences, and preferences provided by employees on application forms. This information has been found to have moderate validity for predicting job performance—provided the questions asked are indeed relevant to the job in question. For example, suppose that a job requires a lot of travel; a question on the application form might ask, "How willing are you to travel on the job?" or "How frequently did you travel in your previous job?" Clearly, applicants who are willing to travel are a better choice than those who express reluctance to travel. But remember: Information collected in this manner is useful only to the extent that it is relevant to the job in question. In addition, certain kinds of questions cannot be asked, either in person or on application forms—questions that inquire about an applicant's personal life, physical characteristics, personal health, prior arrest records, or personal habits can violate Equal Employment Opportunity laws and guidelines and can land an entrepreneur in hot water. As long as questions are focused directly on knowledge, skills, preferences, and experience related to the job, these problems can be avoided and structured interviews can be a valuable tool for choosing the best individuals for specific jobs.

Although we have been emphasizing the use of interviews as a tool for selecting employees, it is important to note that many companies—new ventures included—often use such meetings with job applicants for another purpose: to build the image of the company. Up to a point, this can be a good strategy. But research indicates that it is often a big mistake to oversell a company, whether it is a new start-up or an established corporation. Painting too positive or rosy a picture of working conditions can set employees up for major disappointments once they are on the job, and this can undermine both their motivation and commitment. In general, it is much better to make sure that interviews reflect what are known as realistic job previews—efforts to present a balanced and accurate picture of the company to potential employees. In that way, unpleasant surprises are minimized and new employees are more likely to remain on the job after they are hired.[7]

Why should you want to know about these techniques and procedures? For two reasons, which we have already noted above: (a) You will probably carry out the tasks of recruiting and selecting employees yourself, at least initially, and (b) later on, if you decide to delegate these tasks to others, you should still want to retain oversight, to assure that they are being handled correctly. Remember, not only is recruitment of excellent employees crucial to the future of a new venture, but carrying out this task in an inappropriate manner can put the company at risk for lawsuits. Clearly, this is one more instance where the adage "better safe than sorry" applies—with a vengeance.

One final point: It is absolutely crucial to carefully check all references provided by job applicants and all claims that they make concerning past experience and training. All people, unfortunately, are not completely honest, and applicants for jobs at new ventures are no exception to this general rule. To be on the safe side, entrepreneurs should check at least major aspects of an applicant's resume before hiring this person. In all likelihood, the information is accurate, but in a few cases, there might be some big surprises lurking around the edges!

Motivating Employees: Maximizing the Value of the New Venture's Human Resources

The early hires of a company might be acquaintances, former coworkers, or people referred to the entrepreneurs by close friends, so these individuals might well have high levels of motivation. But once a new venture begins to grow and to hire additional employees, the issue of motivation—of how to motivate these individuals so that they will do their best work—arises just as it does in every other organization. In fact, since every person on the payroll matters to a new venture and it cannot afford to support "free riders" who coast along on the efforts of others, the question "How can employee motivation be maximized?" is a key one for entrepreneurs. In this section, we will offer some concrete suggestions for reaching this goal. Initially, most entrepreneurs use an inspiring vision of what their companies can become to motivate new employees, and they are often highly skilled in this regard.[1] But this is just one technique that might be effective for building motivation, and we believe that it is very useful for entrepreneurs to at least be familiar with several others.

Before turning to these "motivation boosters," however, we should say a few words about just what we mean by the term "motivation." In the fields of human resource management and organizational behavior, the two branches of management that have focused most attention on this topic, motivation is usually defined as the processes that *arouse*, *direct*, and *maintain* human behavior toward attaining some *goal*. In other words, motivation refers to behavior that is energized by, and directed toward, reaching some desired target or objective. All four components are necessary: Nothing happens without arousal (energy), and nothing is accomplished by random flailing around—to attain specific goals, behavior must be directed and generally continued over some period of time.

Here is a simple example: Suppose that an entrepreneur wants to obtain financing for her new venture. She does not sit around daydreaming about this objective; rather she takes active, energetic steps to reach it. And these steps are directed—they are not sheer random activity. For example, she might use her network to identify possible "business angels" or to get her in contact with venture capitalists and other potential sources of funding. She does not, in contrast, go to a nearby intersection with a sign reading, "Need money for a new venture" and try to solicit it from passing motorists. Furthermore, her behavior persists over time; she does not quit after one or two setbacks. On the contrary, her desire to obtain financing is strong, so she continues to try over and over again. Since all four components are present—energy, direction, persistence, and a clear objective or goal, her actions illustrate the basic nature of motivation. Note that this is an example of self-motivation; the entrepreneur is motivated to obtain financing by internal factors—her own goals and desires. Since a key task for entrepreneurs is that of motivating others, we will focus primarily on this issue in the present discussion.

Reaching for the Moon—Or at Least, the Next Level Up: The Key Role of Goals

When you work on a task, do you set goals for yourself? If you are like most ambitious, hard-working people, the answer is probably *yes*. And you probably already know that setting goals in this way can be highly motivating; they can help us to maintain behavior for long periods of time. Why? Partly because knowing where we want to get (our goal) helps us measure our progress; we can tell whether, and how quickly, we are getting where we want to be. And that, it appears, helps us to continue; in fact, research indicates that the closer we get to a specific goal, the stronger our motivation to reach it will become and the greater the effort we expend trying to finally get there.[2]

So far, we have only been talking about the goals people set for themselves. Clearly, many entrepreneurs are masters at this task; in fact, the desire to set their own goals—to have personal control over their lives and their own activities—is one reason why many people become entrepreneurs in the first place.[3] For example, consider Jon Oringer, who recently started a software company (SurfSecret Software).[4] Oringer was a graduate student living comfortably in his parents' home, but he wanted the independence that he believed running his own business would provide. So, he gave up his secure life, moved into his own apartment, and started his company, which now employs four off-site programmers. In some ways, his life is certainly harder than it was in his previous situation; but he now has the personal control he craved, so in his view, the trade-off was a very good one.

In contrast to entrepreneurs, many people are not so self-directed; they do not seek total independence and do not always set goals for themselves. Or if they do, they set goals that are so easy to reach that they are not very motivating. Echoing this basic fact, a vast number of research studies indicate that, in many business contexts, setting goals for employees is an extremely useful way to increase their motivation—and their performance. To be maximally helpful, though, such goals must meet certain criteria:

- They must be challenging. The goals must be a "stretch" for the people involved, so that they have to work hard to expend effort to reach them. In contrast, goals that are not challenging do not increase motivation and performance.
- They must be attainable. Setting impossible goals that people cannot reach does not increase their motivation or performance; on the contrary, it often encourages them to give up since they conclude that they cannot possibly reach the stated objective.
- They must be specific. Just telling people to "do their best" or "increase your output" is practically useless. To motivate increased effort and performance, goals must be specific (e.g., "increase your output by 15% within a month," "reduce your error rate by 20% within two weeks").
- They must be accepted by the people involved. If people reject a goal because it is not consistent with their own wishes or objectives, it will have little if any impact on them; after all, it is not their goal, so why should they try to attain it?

- Feedback concerning progress must be provided. The people involved must be kept informed about how they are doing: Are they moving toward the goal? At an acceptable pace? In the absence of such feedback, people have no idea about whether their efforts are paying off and might soon become discouraged.

As we noted earlier, a large body of evidence suggests that setting goals that meet these criteria is a powerful technique for increasing motivation and performance.[5] Indeed, the results it produces are often nothing short of dramatic. For example, in one recent study, operators of a pizza chain found that drivers who delivered its pizzas were not stopping fully at stop signs, thus putting themselves and the company at risk for accidents—and law suits. Goal setting coupled with concrete feedback was used to change this behavior: Drivers were given the specific goal of coming to a complete stop at least 75% of the time (versus the 45% rate they showed at the beginning of the study). Furthermore, their driving was observed, and they were given feedback about the extent to which they met this goal every week. The results were dramatic: Shortly after goal setting and feedback were instituted, the drivers' performance rose to very close to the target level. However, when feedback was discontinued, their rate dropped back down to what it had been before. (A control group received no goal and no feedback; as expected, their behavior did not change during the course of the study.)

Because goal setting is relatively easy to use, it can be a powerful technique for entrepreneurs. To be effective, though, it must be applied in accordance with the guidelines described above. If these are ignored, results will probably be disappointing.

Throughout this discussion, we have mentioned motivation and performance together. It is important to note that they are definitely not the same thing. Motivation is a key ingredient in the performance of many tasks, but by itself, it is not a guarantee of improved performance. For example, if employees lack required skills or knowledge to perform a job well, they will probably be unable to do so even if their motivation is very high—that is one reason why careful selection of job applicants is so important. Similarly, even highly motivated people might not be able to do a good job with poor or faulty equipment. So keep in mind that motivation is only one of the ingredients in good performance; it is often a crucial one, but it is by no means the entire story.

Tying Rewards to Performance: The Role of Expectancies

In general, people are optimistic; they believe, more than is justified by the cold light of reason, that things will turn out well and that they will experience positive outcomes in many different situations.[6] This tendency is closely related to motivation: Because they are optimistic, people generally believe that the greater the effort they expend on a given task, the better they will perform it, and that good performance will generally yield larger rewards than poor performance. In many cases, these assumptions are reasonable ones; in others, though, they can be misleading. For example, have you ever tried to perform a task with faulty tools or when you were lacking some necessary information? In such cases, working hard does not necessarily improve performance. Take, for example, trying to build a bookcase. If you don't know enough about how pieces of wood can be joined together, it does not matter how hard you work; what you produce will still be pretty shaky.

Similarly, you have probably experienced situations in your life where good performance was not recognized or rewarded; perhaps the situation was unfair, or your good work was just overlooked.

An important theory of motivation known as expectancy theory,[7] suggests that both these factors, plus one more, play a key role in motivation. Specifically, this theory—which has been verified by many different studies—suggests that people will be motivated to work hard on a task only when three conditions prevail: (a) They believe that expending effort will improve their performance (expectancy), (b) they believe that good performance will be rewarded (instrumentality), and (c) they see that the rewards offered are ones they really want or value (valence). When any of these factors is missing, motivation tends to drop to very low levels. This is eminently reasonable. Why, after all, should anyone exert effort on tasks when doing so will not help them to perform better or when there is no link between the quality of one's performance and the payoffs one receives? The answer is clear: Under these conditions, they will not expend the effort—they will not be motivated to work hard on this particular task.

Here is where things get interesting. Many people experience declines in motivation when confronted with poor performance. Thus, in running their new ventures, entrepreneurs should take careful note of this fact. It suggests several practical steps that they can implement to maintain the motivation of their employees at high levels:

- Make sure that effort does indeed lead to good performance—this means assuring that people have the training, equipment, and knowledge they need to perform their jobs well. If these are lacking and effort does not produce improvements in performance, employees might get discouraged, with costly results for the new venture.
- Make sure that good performance is recognized and rewarded—that there is a close link between performance and rewards. This can be done through the reward system of pay, bonuses, and other positive outcomes established for the new venture. When excellent performance is not recognized and rewarded, there is more at work than motivation—there is also the very real possibility that the employees will decide to leave, and that can be devastating for a new venture. (We will return to this in more detail in our discussion of useful steps for retaining first-rate employees.)
- Make sure that the rewards provided for good performance are ones that employees really want. This sounds obvious, but remember that money is not the only thing people want from their jobs. True, it is certainly important to them. But sometimes, people value other outcomes, such as specific kinds of fringe benefits, flexible working hours or vacation schedules, praise and recognition. For example, biotech start-ups often permit their scientists to publish research findings because being able to do so increases the motivation of these highly trained professionals. It is for this reason that organizations are currently offering employees a broad range of benefits. If you

want to hold onto the best people in your company, this is a valuable principle to remember.

In sum, to the extent that the links between effort and performance, or performance and reward, are strong and clear for employees, their motivation will be high. Break or weaken these links, however, and the results might be a demoralized and demotivated workforce. Savvy entrepreneurs, therefore, will take careful note of these basic facts and do everything in their power to assure that conditions favoring high levels of motivation are the standard in their new ventures. Again, if they do not focus on this task themselves, they should be certain that the people to whom they delegate it are using the techniques described above; if they are not, this might be reason for concern—and added oversight.

Fairness: An Essential Ingredient in Motivation

The summer in between his freshman and sophomore years at college, one of the authors of this book, Robert, worked in the finance office of a large labor union. He was a summer fill-in, so the work was completely boring: He mainly filed forms and prepared new file folders by placing labels on them. His hours were long, and he had to punch a time clock when he arrived and when he left. He had only 45 minutes for lunch and one 15-minute break in the morning. He needed the money for college, so he would have gladly put up with all of this except for one thing: Another student also working there was treated much better. Tom, who was a year older than Robert, arrived late every morning and often left early. He disappeared for long periods of time during the day and often took 2-hour lunches. Worst of all, he was given the most interesting jobs to do. The final blow came when, by mistake, Robert received his paycheck. When Robert opened the envelope and discovered that it was 50% higher than his check, his head nearly exploded over the unfairness of it all. "Who the heck is this guy to get such special treatment?" Robert wondered. He soon found out; Tom was the nephew of the president of the union. End of mystery—but not of Robert's feelings of being treated unfairly.

What do you think these feelings of unfairness did to Robert's motivation? As you can readily guess, they caused it to drop to zero. "Why should I put out effort for an organization that treats me like this?" Robert remembers thinking. In fact, this is one of the key effects of unfairness in business contexts; the people exposed to it experience a strong drop in motivation. Even worse, they often engage in instances of theft and sabotage, partly because of their anger toward the business that has treated them unfairly, and partly because this is one way to even the score, so to speak—to get what they feel they deserve, even if they have to take it themselves.[8]

This situation provides a clear illustration of one set of conditions that leads individuals to conclude that they are being treated unfairly—an imbalance between the *contributions* they make and the *outcomes* (rewards) they receive, *relative to those of other people.*[9] In general, we expect this ratio of contributions and rewards to be about the same for everyone in the group: The more each person contributes, the larger the rewards he or she receives. In other words, we seek distributive justice (or *equity*)—conditions under which available rewards are divided fairly among group members, according to what each has contributed to the group.[10] It was the absence of this kind of fairness that upset Robert in his summer job. His contributions were actually *larger* than those of the other student, yet the other student's rewards were greater than Robert's.

An imbalance between what they receive and what they contribute is not the only reason people feel unfairly treated, however. Such feelings can arise when people feel that the procedures in dividing available rewards are not fair (*procedural justice*), or when they feel that the people who distribute these rewards have not explained their decisions adequately or shown enough courtesy in their behavior (*interactional justice*).[11] Reactions to these kinds of injustice, too, are much the same: People become angry, feel resentment, and experience a drop in the desire to work hard. They might also demand larger rewards or more courteous treatment or—ultimately—take a walk and leave this exploitative workplace behind.

What does this mean for entrepreneurs? Several things. First, they should be very careful to be fair to people in their new ventures. This means that strong efforts must be made to link rewards to performance as closely as possible, so that the greater employees' contributions, the greater their rewards. Second, it means that it is important to establish fair procedures for evaluating performance and distributing available rewards—procedures that are understood by all employees. And third, it suggests a strong reason for treating employees with courtesy and respect. Not only is this ethically correct, but it is also an essential condition for maintaining a high level of motivation.

Designing Jobs to Make Them Motivating

We should briefly mention one additional technique for maintaining or increasing motivation among the employees of a new venture: designing the jobs that they perform so that they are intrinsically motivating. Almost no one likes jobs that are totally routine and completely repetitious, and over which they have little or no control. People who find themselves in such jobs become "clock watchers," impatiently waiting for the day to end so that they can get back to their real lives—the things they enjoy and that matter to them. Certainly, their jobs are low on the list.

It is all too easy for entrepreneurs, who are often excited about creating something new and are typically overstimulated every day, to overlook this fact. They forget that employees might not share in these feelings and might, in fact, be bored by the tasks that they perform. This suggests that some attention to job design—to structuring jobs so that they increase people's interest in doing them (and hence their motivation)—is important. Fortunately, reaching this goal is not very difficult. Two basic steps can be very helpful in assuring that employees' jobs are *not* totally routine. One approach is known as *job enlargement*, which involves expanding jobs so that they include a wider variety of tasks and activities. For example, instead of having an employee pack products for shipment all day, this person can also be asked to help keep track of returns and perhaps play a role in ordering supplies needed in shipping.

The second basic technique of job design is *job enrichment*, which involves giving employees not simply more tasks but ones requiring a higher level of skill and responsibility. For example, the boring summer job we described earlier could have been enriched by allowing Robert to answer members' requests for various forms or information booklets.

Those tasks would involve a little more thought than filing endless forms and would also be ones he could do at his own pace.

New ventures have an advantage over large, preexisting companies in which complex and unreliable reward systems and organizational politics often get in the way of ensuring these two job attributes. But these key ingredients in employee motivation will *not* take care of themselves. They will exist only to the extent that entrepreneurs, or others to whom this task has been delegated, take the time to assure their presence. Given the crucial role of employee motivation in the success of a new venture, this is a task entrepreneurs should definitely *not* neglect.

Retaining High-Performing Employees

Good people are always in demand, so new ventures face the same problem that all companies do: how to retain high-performing employees. Doing so is especially crucial for new ventures for two key reasons: (a) Replacing good people requires time and other precious resources that the new venture can ill afford, and (b) when they leave, they might take important information with them—perhaps to competitors! For these reasons, it is truly important for new ventures to retain their key employees. Many strategies can be useful in this regard, but two are most important: (a) developing excellent reward systems and (b) building a high level of commitment and loyalty among employees. These two strategies are related, but because they involve somewhat different actions, we will discuss them separately, taking care to note links between them.

Reward Systems: Linking Pay and Performance

When bright, talented people come to work for a new venture, they are, in essence, taking a risk; such people can always find good jobs in large organizations—ones that offer higher levels of job security. So why do they choose to join relatively risky new ventures? Several factors probably play a role: the commitment and enthusiasm of the founders, who tell a good story about their companies and their potential futures, and dissatisfaction with conditions in the large companies where they worked previously. Another factor that is crucial, and the one on which we will focus here, involves potential rewards: Good people come to work for new ventures because they perceive greater potential for rewards in this setting. If this is so, then assuring that these beliefs are realized—or at least remain viable—is a crucial task for entrepreneurs. How can this goal be attained? The answer is largely through the development of effective reward systems—systems in the new venture for recognizing and rewarding good performance.

In general terms, the kind of systems most suitable for new ventures is described in the field of human resource management as pay-for-performance systems (or *incentive systems*). Such systems assume that employees differ in how much they contribute to the company's success and that they should be rewarded in accordance with the scope of their contributions. In other words, such systems strive for *distributive justice*. Several varieties of such plans exist. The most common type, *merit pay plans*, offer employees an increase in base pay, with the size of the increase being determined by their performance. The higher this is rated to be, the larger the raise. (Space limitations preclude our discussing the complexities involved in measuring and rating employees' performance, but suffice it to say that it is crucial that these tasks be carried out in a systematic and accurate manner. This is far from easy. In fact, this matter is so complex, that we recommend that entrepreneurs hire appropriate consultants to help them establish such systems of performance appraisal.)

Another type of individual pay-for-performance plan involves bonuses. In such plans, employees receive a bonus based, again, on their performance. A variant of these plans involves awards—tangible prizes, such as paid vacations, electronic equipment, or other desirable items. In new ventures, entrepreneurs might also provide either actual stock in the company or *stock options* to employees. The latter give the employees the right to purchase shares of the company at a given price. Research findings indicate that new ventures that provide equity to employees grow faster and attain greater success than those that do not, so this appears to be a very useful technique well worth considering.[1]

All of these pay-for-performance plans can be highly effective if designed and administered carefully. The advantages lie primarily in the fact that such plans translate the principles that we described in our discussion of motivation into tangible actions important to employees. The link between performance and reward is strengthened, commitment to the company's goals is increased, and fairness (in terms of a balance between contributions and outcomes) is obtained. No wonder these plans often work!

Like every management procedure, however, pay-for-performance plans have a downside. Most important among these is the possibility that a "do only what you get paid for" mentality might develop. In other words, employees might focus on whatever indicators of performance are part of the system, while neglecting everything else. For example, in some school systems, teachers' pay has been linked to the scores their students attain on standardized tests. The result? The teachers focus on helping their students do well on these tests (e.g., by learning various test-taking tactics) rather than on helping them understand the subject matter that they are studying. Similarly, the number of "no shows" (passengers who book tickets but do not show up) rose when airlines began compensating reservations agents on the number of reservations they booked.

Another problem with pay-for-performance plans is that they are hard to follow during tough economic times. When funds for raises and bonuses are severely limited—or even nonexistent—it might not be feasible to offer meaningful rewards to employees even for truly outstanding performance. Under these conditions, entrepreneurs need to be creative to hold onto their first-rate employees. People will not work hard forever without tangible rewards, so this, experts suggest, is when effective communication with employees becomes essential. They should be fully informed about the current situation and about the entrepreneurs' plans to help things improve. In the meantime, entrepreneurs should do everything they can to demonstrate that they really do value excellent performance. For example, they can offer nonmonetary support to hard-pressed employees, such as adopting flexible hours and creating a pool of child care resources. The main point is that ambitious, hard-working people can put up with difficult situations—including a gap between their performance and their rewards—on a temporary basis. But to maintain their motivation, it is important to assure them that this state of affairs will not persist. If they conclude that it will not change, their motivation will drop and they will head for the exit as soon as it is feasible.

In contrast to individual pay-for-performance plans, other reward systems offer incentives to teams of employees rather than to individuals. In such plans, all team members receive rewards based on the team's overall performance. This can lead to increased performance and a high level of cohesiveness among group members but is unsatisfying to many people who prefer to float or sink on their own merits. It also encourages free-riding effects in which some team members do most of the work while others ride on their coattails.

Perhaps more useful to new ventures are company-wide pay-for-performance plans, in which all employees share in the company's profits. Profit-sharing plans distribute a portion of the company's earnings to employees, while employee stock ownership plans reward employees with stock or options to purchase the company's stock at a specific (favorable) price. These plans make employees partners in the new venture, and this can work wonders for their motivation—and their desire to remain with the company. We are reminded of this every time we visit a Home Depot. This large corporation has an unusually generous employee stock ownership plan, and it shows in the behavior of employees; almost all are eager and happy to help, and when asked if they like working there, they reply "yes!" with enthusiasm. Moreover, several have gone on to explain to us that they feel strong loyalty to Home Depot, mainly because they feel that they own a share in it themselves.

In sum, instituting an effective and fair reward system is one major technique through which new ventures can retain their best employees. Thus, this is an issue entrepreneurs should consider with care as their new ventures grow and they hire increasing numbers of employees.

Building Employee Commitment

Why do people decide to leave one job for another? The answer is definitely *not* as simple as "because they can earn more money." On the contrary, the decision to leave appears to be a complex one, involving lots of thought and many factors.[2] How, then, can entrepreneurs tip this decision-making process in their favor, so that high-performing employees remain on board? A key factor involves organizational commitment—the extent to which an individual identifies and is involved with his or her organization and is, therefore, unwilling to leave it.[3] High levels of organizational commitment are often present in new ventures, where, at least initially, employees are recruited and hired by the founders. As new ventures grow and this task is delegated to others, however, there is the real risk that such commitment will decrease, so this is an important consideration that entrepreneurs should not overlook.

Actually, three distinct kinds of organizational commitment exist. One, known as *continuance commitment*, refers mainly to the costs of leaving. If an individual would lose a lot by leaving (e.g., some portion of a pension plan, the opportunity to see close friends), this can weigh heavily in the balance and cause him to remain. For example, stock contributions made by companies to retirement funds are nontaxable until employees redeem the stock. This can increase continuance commitment because employees want to remain with the company until the stock rises to high levels. Similarly, stock distributed as part of employee stock ownership plans might not become fully vested for employees until some period of time has elapsed. Again, this can increase continuance commitment. A second kind of commitment is known as *affective commitment*—it refers mainly to positive feelings toward the organization. If an individual shares the values of her or his company and holds it in high regard, this employee is less likely to leave than someone with the opposite feelings. Finally, individuals might remain with a company as a result of *normative commitment*—they stay because of a feeling of obligation to others who would be adversely affected by their departure.

All three of these forms of commitment are important to new ventures, because each tends to help in the retention of employees. Employees of new ventures often identify with them because they believe in what the company is doing—that is why they came there in the first place! So to the extent that such feelings can be strengthened, new ventures can retain their best employees.

Is building a high level of organizational commitment worth the bother? Research findings indicate that it is. The higher employees' commitment, the less likely they are to leave for another job.[4] And that, after all, is what entrepreneurs want—retention of people whom they have worked hard to hire and who are essential to their companies' continued growth.

Overcoming the "Control Barrier":
A Note on the Necessity of "Letting Go"

While many entrepreneurs want to surround themselves with the best people—to hire excellent employees—they often have a very hard time "letting to"—delegating authority to other people.[5] The reasons for this are understandable: Entrepreneurs often have a passion for their companies and view them almost through the eyes of a doting parent. And just like loving parents, they find it difficult to surrender their authority and let other people control their new ventures' fate by making important decisions or setting strategy. Yet—and here is the paradox—unless they can accomplish this task, they might put the future of their growing companies in jeopardy. To understand why, we need to take a brief look at how new ventures grow and move through successive stages of development.

Company growth is a continuous process, so dividing it into discrete phases is somewhat artificial. Still, many experts find it convenient to talk about six different phases through which many companies move:

1. **Conception/Existence**. This is the classic "start-up" phase, during which companies emerge and move toward the point at which they can deliver a product or service. During this phase, founders do essentially everything, so the issue of delegating does not arise.

2. **Survival**. At this stage of development, the new venture has become a real company; it has customers and is earning revenues. During this phase, too, the issue of delegation is relatively unimportant; while there might be a small number of employees, the founders remain central in every aspect of its operation.

3. **Profitability and Stabilization**. During this phase, the company attains economic health; it is earning a profit and has a growing number of employees. Functional managers are hired, but since the company is still small, the founders continue to play a key role and delegation is just beginning to become an important issue.

4. **Profitability and Growth**. At this stage, the company moves toward real growth, and to reach this goal, its growing cash reserves are placed at risk (i.e., they are used to finance further growth). The founders are still central to all aspects of the company's business, but

high-quality managers are needed to oversee its increasingly complex operations.

5. **Takeoff**. This is the pivotal phase of company's growth from the point of view of delegation; the company is growing rapidly and becomes far too large for one founder or even a team of founders to oversee effectively. This necessitates the hiring of first-rate, professional managers—and these people will not come on board, or remain, if they are not given sufficient authority and autonomy to do their jobs. This phase encompasses what some authors term the *control barrier*. The founders must surrender at least a significant amount of control over the company to others—people whom they have hired, bankers, new shareholders who have provided needed capital. If they successfully pass through this barrier, the company can continue to grow; if they do not, its fortunes might begin to decline—a pattern that is far from rare.[6]

6. **Maturity**. If founders successfully navigate their way through the control barrier, the company becomes truly mature; it has, in a sense, arrived and is a significant player in its industry or market.

Here is a key point about these phases: In the early ones (phases 1 and 2), entrepreneurs' skills, abilities, and knowledge—their capacity to accomplish various tasks—are crucial to the success of the company. From the third phase on, however, their importance in determining the success of the company begins to decline. At the same time, though, the importance of another factor—the founders' ability to delegate—increases until the two curves cross; this is the point at which the control barrier occurs. Beyond that point, success at delegating is crucial and, in fact, is closely tied with the company's ability to recruit, motivate, and retain high-quality employees and staff.

What all of this suggests, in essence, is that entrepreneurs must change their style of leadership as their companies grow. At first, they act as team leaders, people who lead a small group of highly motivated people toward shared goals—primarily through the vision that they describe and endorse. Later on, they must become leaders of teams—key decision makers who, nevertheless, delegate a large degree of authority and autonomy to other people who lead various teams within the company, such as separate departments or, perhaps, integrated cross-functional teams. Whatever form the growing organization takes, founders must truly let go—delegating authority and recruiting, motivating, and retaining first-rate people. Once they are on board, it is only reasonable for entrepreneurs to entrust them with key tasks; if this does not occur, why should these talented, energetic people stay around? The answer is simple: They will not. So letting go in an orderly manner, and at the appropriate point in time, is one of the best things founding entrepreneurs can do for their companies. And this is another reason why paying careful attention to recruiting, motivating, and retaining first-rate employees is crucial to the success of new ventures; when entrepreneurs do a good job at these tasks and are surrounded by truly excellent people, the pain of letting go might be significantly reduced. After all, they realize that they are placing the fortunes of their companies in very good hands!

Some Concluding Thoughts

Many companies—and new ventures are no exception to this generalization—proudly proclaim that "our people are our most precious resource." In other words, they recognize that the knowledge, skills, talents, and commitment supplied by employees are the most important ingredients in the company's success—or failure. A vast body of evidence in the field of human resources suggests that this is true: People are a crucial factor in determining the success of any business, large preexisting ones and small start-ups alike.[1] Indeed, they are just as important in this respect as technological, legal, and financial factors. For this reason, it is very important that the founders of new ventures devote careful attention to the issues considered here—hiring excellent employees, carefully determining the optimal size of the company's workforce, and attaining a good balance between temporary and permanent human resources, among other things. Lack of attention to these issues can prove as deadly to the new company's fortunes as beginning with a mismatched founding team or allowing working relations between members of this team to deteriorate to the point where they become ineffective. Excellent human resources, in short, are an essential part of the foundation of new ventures, and as we are sure you will agree, only structures that are built on firm foundations endure.

Notes

Similarity Versus Complementarity

1. Byrne, D. (1991). Perspectives on research classics: This ugly duckling has yet to become a swan. *Contemporary Social Psychology, 15*, 84–85.

2. Greenberg, J., & Baron, R. A. (2003). *Behavior in organizations* (8th ed.). Upper Saddle River, NJ: Prentice-Hall.

3. Erikson, T. (2002). Entrepreneurial capital: The emerging venture's most important asset and competitive advantage. *Journal of Business Venturing, 17*, 275–290.

4. Keller, R. T. (2000). Cross-functional project groups in research and new product development: Diversity, communications, job stress, and outcomes. *Academy of Management Journal, 44*, 547–555.

Choosing Cofounders

1. Baron, R. A., & Byrne, D. (2002). *Social psychology* (10th ed.). Boston: Allyn & Bacon.

2. Baron, R. A., & Markman, G. (2003). Beyond social capital: The role of entrepreneurs' social competence in their financial success. *Journal of Business Venturing, 18*, 41–60; Baron & Markman. (in press). Entrepreneurs social skills and new venture performance: Mediating mechanisms and cultural generality. *Journal of Management.*

3. Ferris, G. R., Witt, L. A., & Hockhwarter, W. Q. (2001). Interaction of social skill and general mental ability on job performance and salary. *Journal of Applied Psychology, 86*, 1075–1082.

4. Terry, R. L., & Krantz, J. H. (1993). Dimensions of trait attributions associated with eyeglasses, men's facial hair, and women's hair length. *Journal of Applied Social Psychology, 23*, 1757–1769.

5. Baron and Markman, Beyond social capital.

6. Kilduff, M., & Day, D. V. (1994). Do chameleons get ahead? The effects of self-monitoring on managerial careers. *Academy of Management Journal, 37*, 1047–1060.

7. Wayne, S. J., & Ferris, G. R. (1990). Influence tactics and exchange quality in supervisor-subordinate interactions: A laboratory experiment and field study. *Journal of Applied Psychology, 75*, 487–499.

8. Olson, J. M., Hafer, C. L., & Taylor, L. (2001). I'm mad as hell and I'm not going to take it anymore: Reports of negative emotions as a self-presentation tactic. *Journal of Applied Social Psychology, 31*, 981–999.

9. Wayne, S. J., Liden, R. C., Graf, I. K., & Ferris G. R. (1997). The role of upward influence tactics in human resource decisions. *Personnel Psychology, 50*, 979–1006.

10. Vonk, R. (1998). The slime effect: Suspicion and dislike of likeable behavior toward superiors. *Journal of Personality and Social Psychology, 74*, 849–864.

11. Ensley, M. D., Pearson, A. W., & Amason, A. C. (2002). Understanding the dynamics of new venture top management teams: Cohesion, conflict, and new venture performance. *Journal of Business Venturing, 17*, 365–386.

12. Byrne, D. (1991). Perspectives on research classics: This ugly duckling has yet to become a swan. *Contemporary Social Psychology, 15*, 84–85.

13. Cropanzano, R. D. (Ed.). (1993). *Justice in the workplace*. Hillsdale, NJ: Erlbaum.

14. Brown, J. D., & Rogers, R. J. (1991). Self-serving attribution: The role of physiological arousal. *Personality and Social Psychology Bulletin, 17*, 501–506.

15. Grote, N. K., & Clark, M. S. (2001). Perceiving unfairness in the family: Cause of consequences of marital distress? *Journal of Personality and Social Psychology, 80*, 281–289.

16. Tjosvold, D. (1993). *Learning to manage conflict: Getting people to work together productively*. New York: Lexington Books.

17. Personal correspondence.

18. Baron, R. A. (1993). Criticism (informal negative feedback) as a source of perceived unfairness in organizations: Effects, mechanisms, and countermeasures. In R. Cropanzano (Ed.), *Justice in the workplace: Approaching fairness in human resource management* (pp. 155–170). Hillsdale, NJ: Erlbaum.

19. Thompson, L. (1998). *The mind and heart of the negotiator*. Upper Saddle River, NJ: Prentice-Hall.

Expanding the New Venture's Human Resources

1. Schefcyzk, M., & Gerpott, T. J. (2001). Qualifications and turnover of managers and venture capital-financed firm performance: An empirical study of German venture capital-investments. *Journal of Business Venturing, 16*, 145–165.

2. Eisenhardt, K., & Schoonhoven, K. (1995). Failure of entrepreneurial firms: Ecological, upper echelons and strategic explanations in the U.S. semiconductor industry. Working Paper, Stanford University.

3. Reynolds, P., & White, S. (1997). *The entrepreneurial process: Economic growth, men, women and minorities*. Westport, CT: Quorum Books.

4. Aldrich, H. (1999). *Organizations evolving*. London: Sage.

5. Baum, J. (1996). Organizational ecology. In S. Clegg, C. Hardy, & W. Nord (Eds.), *Handbook of organization studies* (pp. 77–114). London: Sage.

6. Shutjens, V., & Wever, E. (2000). Determinants of new firm success. *Papers in Regional Science, 79*, 135–159.

7. Gimeno, J., Folta, T., Cooper, A., & Woo, C. (1997). Survival of the fittest? Entrepreneurial human capital and the persistence of underperforming firms. *Administrative Science Quarterly, 42*, 750–783.

8. Matusik, S. (1997). Motives, use patterns and effects of contingent resource use in entrepreneurial firms. In P. Reynolds, W. Bygrave, N. Carter, P. Davidsson, W. Gartner, C. Mason, & P. McDougall (Eds.), *Frontiers of entrepreneurship research* (pp. 359–372). Babson Park, MA: Babson College.

9. Aldrich, H., & Langdon, N. (1997). Human resource management and organizational life cycles. In P. Reynolds, W. Bygrave, N. Carter, P. Davidsson, W. Gartner, C. Mason, & P. McDougall (Eds.), *Frontiers of entrepreneurship research* (pp. 349–357). Babson Park, MA: Babson College.

Recruiting and Selecting High-Performing Employees

1. Buckley, M. R., & Eder, R. W. (1988). B. M. Springbett and the notion of the "snap decision" in the interview. *Journal of Management, 14*, 59–67.

2. Aldrich, H. (1999). *Organizations evolving*. London: Sage.

3. Eder, R. W., & Ferris, G. R. (Eds.). (1989). *The employment interview: Theory, research, and practice*. Newbury Park, CA: Sage.

4. Gomez-Mejia, L., Balkin, D. B., & Cardy, R. L. (2001). *Managing human resources* (3rd ed.). Upper Saddle River, NJ: Prentice-Hall

5. Kacmar, K. M., Ratcliff, S. L., & Ferris, G. R. (1989). Employment interview research: Internal and external validity. In R. W. Eder & G. R. Ferris (Eds.), *The employment interview: Theory, research, and practice* (pp. 32–41). Newbury Park, CA: Sage.

6. Baron, R. A., & Byrne, D. (2002). *Social psychology* (10th ed.). Boston: Allyn & Bacon.

7. Breaugh, J. A. (1983). Realistic job previews: A critical appraisal and future research directions. *Academy of Management Review, 8*(4): 612–619.

Motivating Employees

1. Churchill, N. (2000). Managing growth. In S. Birley & D. F. Muzyka (Eds.), *Mastering entrepreneurship* (pp. 251–257). Upper Saddle River, NJ: Prentice.

2. Locke, E. A., & Latham, G. P. (1990). *Goal setting*. Englewood Cliffs, NJ: Prentice-Hall.

3. Baron, R. A. (in press). The cognitive perspective: A valuable tool for answering entrepreneurship's basic "why?" questions. *Journal of Business Venturing*.

4. Pennington, A. Y. (2003, March). On a shoestring. *Entrepreneur*, 96.

5. Ludwig, T. D., & Geller, E. S. (1997). Assigned versus participative goal setting and response generalization: Managing injury control among professional pizza deliverers. *Journal of Applied Psychology, 82*, 253–261.

6. Shepperd, J. A., Ouellette, J. A., & Fernandez, J. K. (1996). Abandoning unrealistic optimistic performance estimates and the temporal proximity of self-relevant feedback. *Journal of Personality and Social Psychology, 70*, 844–855.

7. Mitchell, T. R. (1983). Expectancy-value models in organizational psychology. In N. Feather (Ed.), *Expectancy, incentive, and action* (pp. 293–314). Hillsdale, NJ: Lawrence Erlbaum.

8. Greenberg, J. (1998). The cognitive geometry of employee theft: Negotiating "the line" between taking and stealing. In. R. W. Griffin, A. O'Leary-Kelly, & J. M. Collins (Eds.), *Dysfunctional behavior in organizations: Non-violent dysfunctional behavior* (pp. 147–194). Stamford, CT: JAI Press.

9. Brockner, J., & Wiesenfeld, B. M. (1996). An integrative framework for explaining reactions to decisions: The interactive effects of outcomes and procedures. *Psychological Bulletin, 120*, 189–208.

10. Brockner, J., & Wiesenfeld, B. M. (1996). An integrative framework for explaining reactions to decisions: The interactive effects of outcomes and procedures. *Psychological Bulletin, 120*, 189–208.

11. Greenberg, J. (1997). *The quest for justice on the job.* Thousand Oaks, CA: Sage.

Retaining High-Performing Employees

1. Byrne, D. (1991). Perspectives on research classics: This ugly duckling has yet to become a swan. *Contemporary Social Psychology, 15*, 84–85.

2. Mitchell, T. R., & Lee. T. W. (2001). The unfolding model of voluntary turnover and job embeddedness: Foundations for a comprehensive theory of attachment. In B. M. Staw & R. I. Sutton (Eds.), *Research in organizational behavior* (Vol. 23, pp. 189–246). Oxford: Elsevier

3. Meyer, J. P., & Allen, N. J. (1997). *Commitment in the workplace: Theory, research, and application.* Thousand Oaks, CA: Sage.

4. Lee, T. W., Ashford, S. J., Walsh, J. P., & Mowday, R. T. (1992). Commitment propensity, organizational commitment, and voluntary turnover: A longitudinal study of organizational entry processes. *Journal of Management, 18*, 15–32.

5. Churchill, N. C., & Lewis, V. L. (1983, May–June). The five stages of small business growth. *Harvard Business Review, 61*, 2–11.

6. Byrne, Perspectives on research classics.

Some Concluding Thoughts

1. Gomez-Mejia, L. R., Balkin, D. B., & Cardy, R. L. (2002). *Managing human resources* (3rd ed.). Upper Saddle River, NJ: Prentice-Hall.

Index

www.ingramcontent.com/pod-product-compliance
Lightning Source LLC
Chambersburg PA
CBHW071121210326
41519CB00020B/6373